Florence Nightingale
and the
Advancement of Nursing

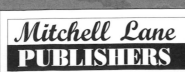

Mitchell Lane
PUBLISHERS

P.O. Box 196
Hockessin, Delaware
19707

Uncharted, Unexplored, and Unexplained

Scientific Advancements of the 19th Century

Titles in the Series

Visit us on the web: www.mitchelllane.com
Comments? email us: mitchelllane@mitchelllane.com

Uncharted, Unexplored, and Unexplained

Scientific Advancements of the 19th Century

Florence Nightingale
and the
Advancement of Nursing

by Bonnie Hinman

Uncharted, Unexplored, and Unexplained

Scientific Advancements of the 19th Century

Printing   1   2   3   4   5   6   7   8
        Library of Congress Cataloging-in-Publication Data

    Florence Nightingale and the advancement of nursing/ Bonnie Hinman.
        p. m. – (Uncharted, unexcplored & unexplained: scientific advancements of the 19th
        century)
    Includes bibliographical references and index.
        Contents: The experiment – The independent thinker – The superintendent – The lady
        with the lamp – A long and useful life.
        ISBN 1-58415-257-5 (lib. bdg.)
1. Nightingale, Florence, 1820 – 1910 – Juvenile literature. 2. Nurses – England – Biography
Juvenile literature. [1. Nightingale Florence, 1820 – 1910. 2. Nurses. 3. Women - Biography.]
I. Title. II. Uncharted, unexplored & unexplained.
RT37.N5H55 2005
610. 73 092 – dc22

                                                                    2003024126

ABOUT THE AUTHOR: Bonnie Hinman has been writing children's books for six years and has been a writer for almost 30 years. Her children's biographies include *Tony Blair, Benjamin Banneker*, and *General Thomas Gage* (Chelsea House). She lives in Joplin, Missouri, with her husband, Bill, two cats, and an energetic black lab dog named Murphy.

PUBLISHER'S NOTE: This story is based on the author's extensive research, which she believes to be accurate. Documentation of such research is contained on page 46-47.

    The internet sites referenced herein were active as of the publication date. Due to the fleeting nature of some web sites, we cannot guarantee they will all be active when you are reading this book.

Uncharted, Unexplored, and Unexplained

Scientific Advancements of the 19th Century

Florence Nightingale
and the Advancement of Nursing

*For Your Information

When Florence visited the front line hospitals at Balaclava in May 1855, the soldiers were thrilled. She was already famous for her nursing work, and the men loved her even more when she rode in a carriage from one battle line to another to talk with them.

1

The Experiment

The rain poured and the wind shrieked as Florence Nightingale and her party of thirty-eight nurses traveled the last miles of the long journey from England to Turkey. Stormy seas had tossed their small steamship, the *Vectis*, during most of its eight-day voyage from Marseilles through the Mediterranean Sea and across the Aegean Sea. A seasick Florence Nightingale must have been relieved to see the ancient city of Constantinople rise up out of the heavy rain as the *Vectis* sailed through the Bosporus Strait on November 4, 1854.

The huge yellow building sitting on top of a hill across the Bosporus from Constantinople would claim the next year and a half of her life and make her a heroine in Great Britain. The building might have looked majestic when the sun briefly touched its yellow stones as the *Vectis* came closer. The illusion didn't last long.

Sailors helped Florence and the nurses climb down into small boats that took them to shore. They landed in Scutari, a suburb of Constantinople. It had been taken over by the British to house sick and wounded soldiers from the Crimean War. A cold wind blew as the nurses scrambled up a muddy, rutted trail that was littered with trash to the Barrack Hospital, the yellow building they had seen from a distance.

Inside, everything was dirty and damp. The long hallways, with broken floor tiles and moldy walls, stood empty of furniture. A courtyard in the center of the building showed only mud and more trash. It was not a promising sight.

Just as bad, five small rooms and a kitchen in a corner tower of the hospital were all that the doctors offered the nurses. One of the rooms even contained a dead body. It turned out to be a Russian general. The corpse was hastily removed.

The uneasy group bedded down that night on hard wooden pallets since there were no beds. The kitchen didn't have a table or any food. Water was limited to two cups a day for washing and drinking. It was not a good start for the grand experiment of sending female nurses to work in British hospitals in the Crimean War.

The conflict pitted Great Britain and France as allies of Turkey against Russia. Russia had destroyed the Turkish fleet late in 1853. The British and French entered the conflict early the following year to keep Russia from gaining control of the Bosporus and the Dardanelles, another Turkish strait less than 100 miles further west. The two straits were the only exit for the large Russian fleet that was based in the Black Sea. The British wanted to keep the Russians bottled up to assure their control of the Mediterranean Sea. Their primary goal in the war became the capture of the large Russian naval base at Sevastopol. It was located on the Crimean Peninsula, where nearly all the fighting would take place.

From the very beginning of the war, the British were plagued by supply problems. It was difficult enough to send supplies and troops from England, and mismanagement caused the chaos. Many shiploads of supplies never arrived at their intended destinations. Inadequately equipped troops suffered many hardships.

William Russell, a reporter for *The Times* newspaper, caused an uproar at home when he reported on the conditions in the Crimea. He also continued by reporting that the French had much better medical

This drawing shows the famous war correspondent, William Russell, seated at a small table writing dispatches to his newspaper. Outside his flimsy tent Florence stands in the snow waiting for the arrival of more wounded and sick soldiers.

arrangements and the help of the Sisters of Charity, a group of nuns who were excellent nurses.

The next day a letter in *The Times* demanded, "Why have we no Sisters of Charity?"[1] This brought a public outcry for female nurses to care for the wounded and sick soldiers. Men called orderlies were doing all of the nursing in the army. They were untrained but did their best under awful circumstances. Decent nursing care was impossible without adequate supplies and equipment.

The government decided to undertake an experiment to stop the soldiers' suffering. Florence Nightingale was asked to lead a party of nurses to Turkey to provide the care that was lacking. She quickly re-cruited a few hospital nurses and a larger group from three religious

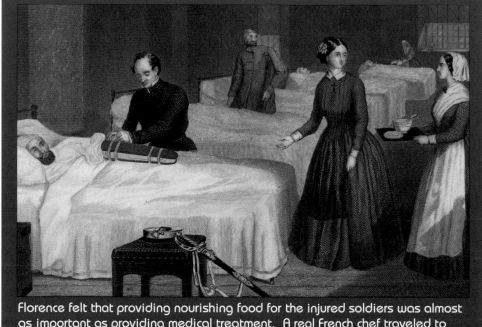

Florence felt that providing nourishing food for the injured soldiers was almost as important as providing medical treatment. A real French chef traveled to Scutari to help Florence give the patients better food. Alex Soyer redesigned the hospital kitchen system, including the ovens, so that fresh soft bread could be baked.

orders. She announced strict rules for the nurses and had uniforms sewn for them. In less than a week they were on their way to the Crimea.

After an uncomfortable first night in their new home, the nurses were eager to get to work. Sick and wounded soldiers were everywhere. One glance told the nurses that there was plenty of work to be done.

The Barrack Hospital had been converted from a Turkish army barracks into a hospital. It would house the flood of wounded and sick soldiers shipped back from the front lines 300 miles away across the Black Sea. But the building was totally unsuited for its new purpose.

Ventilation was nonexistent in the hundreds of small rooms and the privy toilets didn't work. Florence later told the Royal Commission, "It is impossible to describe the state of the atmosphere of the Barrack Hospital at night."[2] She added that she had been in the worst parts of many big cities but the smells in the hospital were even worse.

Florence presented herself to the medical officer in charge to formally offer the nurses' services. To her great surprise, he told her that they were not needed. The doctors had not been consulted about bringing the nurses to Scutari. They didn't intend to let a thirty-four-year-old society lady come into their hospital and tell them what to do.

Florence offered no complaint. She knew that nothing could be accomplished if she didn't have the support of the doctors. She would wait for the medical staff to ask for help.

She retreated to their quarters and set the nurses to work making shirts, stump pillows, and slings, using supplies that she had purchased in Marseilles. It was a good plan for long-term success, but the nurses had to stand by and watch sick and wounded soldiers suffer and die. They might have been willing to endure this if Florence had explained her plan, but she didn't. She simply instructed them to ignore the moans

In spite of the careful nursing that Florence and her nurses gave to the injured and sick soldiers, the death rate continued to be very high. After the Sanitary Commission supervised clean-up work, it was noted that the men lying in beds near the sewer openings had died more frequently than men whose beds were elsewhere.

of the wounded. The nurses obeyed but some resented Florence for what they saw as callous behavior.

The real war provided the ultimate attitude-changing events for the doctors. Wounded and sick soldiers began flooding into Scutari on November 9 after the Battle of Balaclava, which had been fought on October 25. This battle included the famous Charge of the Light Brigade. Another battle at Inkerman two weeks later produced even more casualties.

It was the last straw for the overworked doctors and their orderlies. They desperately needed help. They summoned the nurses, who immediately set to work. Their week's rest was the last any of them would have for a long time.

The First
War Correctpondent

The London newspaper, *The Times*, assigned reporter William Howard Russell to travel with British forces when they departed in February, 1854, for the Crimean Peninsula in Russia. Russell's boss told the eager reporter, "You will be back at Easter, depend upon it, and you will have a pleasant trip."[3] In fact it was two years before the poorly planned and executed war was over.

William Russell

Russell made many enemies by reporting what he saw on the battlefield and behind the lines. He wrote of the mismanagement that led to terrible suffering for the soldiers. His reporting about the wounded and sick led directly to the government sending Florence Nightingale and her nurses to Turkey.

Russell's reporting of one of Britain's most famous losses occurred after the Battle of Balaclava on October 25, 1854. After the disastrous Charge of the Light Brigade in that battle, where more than half of the 673 men were killed or wounded, Russell wrote, "We could scarcely believe the evidence of our senses. Surely that handful of men were not going to charge an enemy in position?"[4]

His dispatches throughout the fall and winter of 1854 and 1855 began to make problems for him and for the British government. The Times readers became angry at the way the war was being run. Attempts by government officials to keep Russell from reporting failed. In January, 1855, Prime Minister G.H. Gordon, the Earl of Aberdeen, resigned because British citizens blamed him for the mess in the Crimea. Russell's reports played a big part in Gordon's downfall and in the replacement of two Crimean army commanders.

It was the first time that a reporter and his newspaper had such an effect on government policy, but it wouldn't be the last.

Florence was five when the family moved into their new home, Embley Park, in Hampshire. Parthe and Florence lived near many cousins and they all spent their time in a flurry of visits. They had pets, played games, and took excursions to nearby points of interest.

2

The Independent Thinker

Florence Nightingale was born in Italy on May 12, 1829. Her parents, Fanny and William Edward Nightingale (or W.E.N. as he was often called), had been traveling in Europe since their marriage almost two years earlier. They had already produced one daughter the year before. She was named Parthenope (pronounced Par-THEN-oh-pea) after an ancient Greek settlement near her birthplace of Naples, Italy. The new baby was named after the beautiful Italian city of Florence.

The girls' parents were members of England's upper class. W.E.N. had inherited a great deal of money and property from an uncle. As members of the upper class, there were many unwritten "rules" to follow. The most important one was that they couldn't work. Gentlemen man-aged their property. They could also hold important positions in the government, army or church. A young woman's primary obligation was to marry well and produce several children.

The Nightingales finally returned to England when Florence was a year old. W.E.N. would have been content to stay in Europe indefinitely, but Fanny was more ambitious. She wanted to have a fine house, give parties frequently, and do a bit of charity work.

Fanny's plans required a grand new home. W.E.N. designed a beautiful mansion with fifteen bedrooms, a stone-terraced garden, and a fine view of a river. It was located on family property in Derbyshire in the middle of England, about 100 miles north of London. They named it

Lea Hurst after two poetic terms: lea means "meadow" and hurst means "low hill."

Lea Hurst was Florence's first true home and remained her favorite, but Fanny soon felt differently about the new house. Situated in the country, it was rather remote and too small for the entertaining that Fanny planned. It was also too cold in the winter. She decided that they would keep Lea Hurst for a summer home but buy a larger property closer to London.

In 1825 the Nightingales moved into Embley Park, near England's southern coast. The new home was huge, and the grounds of the estate covered 4,000 acres. It was also close to Fanny's married sisters and their families. Before long there were many cousins for Florence and Parthe to play with.

Florence's childhood days quickly fell into a routine. In the summer the family traveled north to Lea Hurst, which was near W.E.N.'s family. Late fall, winter, and early spring found the Nightingales at Embley Park. They spent spring and early fall in London for the social seasons.

Fanny had nine brothers and sisters and most of them traded visits constantly. W.E.N. only had a sister, Mai, but she married Fanny's younger brother Sam so the family ties were made even closer. They all loved children, which made childhood special for the Nightingales and their cousins.

Life wasn't always wonderful for Florence, who was often sickly. Illness was a daily fact of life in the first half of the nineteenth century, even for the upper classes. There were few effective treatments for most ailments and little knowledge of the causes of disease.

At first, Florence did her lessons at home with a governess. Then W.E.N. taught both of his daughters. He held advanced views on education for girls, and Florence benefited from her father's attitudes. She learned languages, history, classics and mathematics.

Fanny didn't hold the same modern views as her husband. She loved her daughters very much but never understood that there was any need for all that education. Even so, Fanny was content to let their father decide what the girls should be taught. Besides, it quickly became apparent that Parthe shared Fanny's love of entertaining. W.E.N. and Florence might be in the library discussing Shakespeare, but Parthe had usually slipped away to the drawing room to help her mother plan their next party.

Florence's young life seemed to have all the comfort, love, and learning that a person could hope for. Yet from an early age she was often unhappy. She believed herself to be different from everyone around her and became afraid that this difference would be discovered and condemned.

Florence knew that she wanted to do something important in the world but had no notion what that might be. She later wrote in an autobiographical note, "I craved for some regular occupation, for something worth doing instead of frittering time away on useless trifles."[1] This craving led her to escape more and more often into a dream world.

Florence's emotional ups and downs seem unusual for such an intelligent and realistic young woman. Yet her tendency to exaggerate and to be abnormally sensitive to every slight was quite normal for a young woman living in the romantic age of the nineteenth century. A woman was not considered to be a lady unless she was delicate. Their maids carried smelling salts to revive them when they fainted—which happened often.

The year she was sixteen was an important one for Florence. Fanny had convinced W.E.N. that Embley Park needed remodeling. Fanny proposed that the family visit Europe while the work was being done. The girls would soon be taking their places in formal society, and Fanny thought that some European polish was needed.

Preparations for the trip took months. W.E.N. designed a special traveling coach with three pairs of horses for the family's comfort. There were dozens of letters to and from family members as destinations and possible attractions were suggested and discussed endlessly.

In the midst of this flurry of family activity, Florence experienced something that would shape the rest of her life. In one of her hundreds of notes and journal entries, she described her experience: "On February 7, 1837, God spoke to me and called me to his service."[2]

Florence had no idea yet what that service might be, but she was certain that God would eventually let her know. In the meantime, she entered one of the happiest times of her young life.

The family set off for Europe in September, 1837. For the next year and a half Florence's days were filled with sightseeing, with concerts and parties in the evenings. She met many important people and discovered that she loved music and dancing.

She seemed to have left her recent unhappiness behind. She was full of fun and popular with young men and women. In the midst of the social whirl, Florence found time to study. She kept many notes about the journey, recording in detail the people and places she saw as the family traveled about France, Italy, and Switzerland.

At last they found their way to Paris. Florence met Mary Clarke, who became a good friend. "Clarkey," as she was called, was a famous hostess who gave dinner parties that attracted the most brilliant men in Paris. She took the Nightingales all over Paris to meet famous people, attend the opera, and go to balls.

The Nightingales returned to England in April, 1839. They stayed in London for several months because the Embley Park remodeling wasn't finished. Several of Florence's cousins were also there for the Season. They embarked on another round of social events and were presented to Queen Victoria.

The Nightingales returned to a still-unfinished Embley Park in the fall. Florence kept busy at first helping her mother and sister get the household in order. But by the beginning of 1840, her old unhappiness had returned. She thought her life was pointless and selfish. She also felt guilty that she lived in luxury while others living around her had so little.

The only activities that lifted her unhappiness were nursing family members through illnesses or visiting the cottages around Embley Park and Lea Hurst. She brought food, clothes, and medicines to the poor cottagers and sometimes nursed them through their final illnesses. When Florence was in London, she was also allowed to be a volunteer teacher in a Ragged School for poor children.

These activities were as close to an occupation as Florence was allowed to have. She fretted over the call that she had received almost two years earlier. Why hadn't God let her know what her specific calling would be? Sometimes she wondered if she were doing something wrong that kept God from guiding her. Would she ever be able to begin a real life of purpose and action?

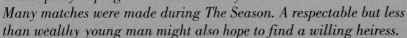

During the Victorian era, English ladies and gentlemen spent much of spring and early summer in London for "The Season." This was a period lasting for several weeks when wealthy and important people flocked to the capital to attend dozens of parties and events. Business contacts were made, but the most important contacts were matrimonial ones. Mothers paraded their daughters to every possible ball and dinner party hoping to attract a wealthy bachelor. Many matches were made during The Season. A respectable but less than wealthy young man might also hope to find a willing heiress.

The imagination and wealth of the host or hostess were all that limited the types of entertainment. There were dinner parties with numerous courses of food where each person's place at the table was carefully planned. There were huge balls, which were only considered a real success if a guest could barely move on the dance floor without running into another dancer. There were musical evenings and amateur theatricals. Card games were popular and charades was a much-loved pastime.

Food and drink were an important part of all of the entertainment. The abundance of wine and elaborate dishes was considered an indication of the success of a party.

Every Victorian mother longed for her daughter to be considered "the life of the party." Social success was invaluable for finding a suitable husband. If a daughter didn't "take," as the ladies were likely to say of a young woman who didn't create a favorable stir, her mother would despair. It wasn't important if the girl herself found the social scene to be tedious, filled as it was with the same people, foods, and events every night. Only a truly rebellious young woman would dare to go against the social customs of The Season.

Florence looks older than her mid-thirties in this portrait. It was fashionable to look quite serious in a picture in those days.

3

The Superintendent

The years passed as Florence moved from Embley Park to London to Lea Hurst and back again. The constant social round left her exhausted and in despair. When she was 24 she finally began to think she knew what God had called her to do. She wanted to help sick people and do it in a better way than simply taking them soup and holding their hands while they died.

She didn't immediately describe her proposed career as nursing. In 1845 nursing wasn't a respectable profession. If medical practices and discoveries lagged behind other sciences at that time, then nursing was downright primitive. A hospital nurse's social status was below that of the lowest housemaid and usually with good reason.

A hospital nurse was a caretaker for the very poor who were sick and had no person to care for them in their homes. Nobody who had any choice went to the hospital when he or she was sick. The nurses were uneducated, underpaid and usually dirty. They had miserable conditions to work in and often drank liquor while on duty. Worst of all, there was a good chance of coming down with a contagious disease. It wasn't an occupation that any respectable woman would want.

Even so, Florence realized that nursing was the name for her calling. Her parents and sister exploded when Florence announced that she wanted to train at a nearby hospital as a nurse. The Nightingales were shocked and wasted no time in crushing Florence's dreams. She was miserable.

Florence may have lost the first battle, but she wasn't about to give up. In spite of her unhappiness, she found ways to learn more and more about sickness and hospitals. Without letting her family know, she had friends send her official reports and other information about health arrangements in England. She studied death rates and sanitation reports from Europe.

She also learned of a nursing school in Kaiserswerth, Germany. It was perfectly respectable, a combined teachers college, prison, orphanage, and hospital. How could her parents refuse her request to travel there to study nursing? Yet she didn't ask them and suffered her lost dreams in silence.

Florence's first glimmer of hope appeared in the fall of 1847 when some older friends, Charles and Selina Bracebridge, invited her to spend the winter in Rome with them. She was able to leave behind some of her misery and enjoy the trip.

During this trip she met Sidney and Elizabeth Herbert. They were rich, yet quite down-to-earth and committed to charity work. Hospital reform was a special interest to them. Florence found willing ears to listen to her developing ideas about hospitals and nursing.

The return home was difficult because nothing had changed there. Florence's family still assumed she would accept the life that they had planned for her.

By the fall of 1849 Florence's mind wandered constantly, and sometimes she didn't even know what was going on around her. In the midst of her despair, a faithful suitor, Richard Monckton Miles, asked for a final decision about marrying him. He had waited for Florence for several years, but now he wanted a firm answer.

After much agonizing, Florence decided that she couldn't give her whole self to marriage and children and still pursue her dreams. She loved Richard and deeply regretted that she had to let him go. He was a close friend and seemed to understand her need to accomplish something in the world.

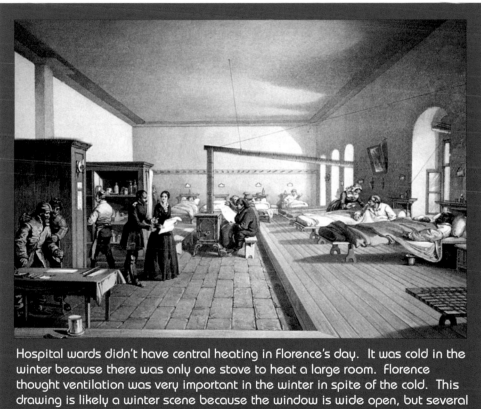

Hospital wards didn't have central heating in Florence's day. It was cold in the winter because there was only one stove to heat a large room. Florence thought ventilation was very important in the winter in spite of the cold. This drawing is likely a winter scene because the window is wide open, but several patients are huddled around a stove.

Her parents reacted with irritation, and Florence sank ever deeper into depression. She became ill with headaches and a cough. Once more the Bracebridges rescued their friend. They proposed that Florence should go with them on a long trip to Egypt and Greece.

This time travel didn't stop Florence's misery. She did the usual sightseeing and even traveled down the Nile River. Yet on her birthday she wrote in her diary, "Today I am 30—the age Christ began his mission. Now no more childish things. No more love. No more marriage. Now Lord let me think only of Thy Will, what Thou willest me to do. Oh Lord Thy Will, Thy Will."[1]

The Bracebridges were alarmed at her mental and physical state so they took a bold step. They took her to Kaiserswerth in Germany. She visited the institution for two weeks to look around and help where needed. When she left Kaiserswerth, her spirits and health were renewed.

She returned home to discover that her mother had found out about the visit to Kaiserswerth and was furious. Parthe was hysterical, and W.E.N. didn't support Florence. Her request to go back to Germany for training was firmly denied. She would stay home and take up the role of society lady that was her rightful place.

The next year was full of anguish for Florence. In a later note she wrote, "In my 31st year I see nothing desirable but death."[2] As unhappy as Florence was, this period served a purpose. It firmed her resolve to change her life, and at last she told her family that she was going back to Germany for training whether they agreed or not.

Fanny saw that Florence would not back down and resentfully gave in. The mother and her two daughters would travel to Europe together. Florence would go to Kaiserswerth while Fanny and Parthe took a water treatment at a spa. Fanny hoped to keep her daughter's odd behavior hidden from friends in this way.

The three months Florence spent at Kaiserswerth made her know absolutely that nursing was the calling that God had told her about so many years before. She lived simply with the other nurses, ate sparingly, and worked long hours. The training itself was basic, and Florence already had studied much of it. But she took many notes and watched carefully how the hospital was managed.

Florence received high praise from the hospital staff and back at home she nursed several family members through illnesses. She tried twice to go to Paris for further training. Each time a family member became seriously ill and required Florence's nursing services.

Then Florence got a real opportunity to make a life for herself. In the spring of 1853, Elizabeth Herbert helped her to be offered a job as superintendent of the Harley Street Hospital, a charity hospital for poor gentlewomen. Though it was a respectable position, Fanny and Parthe were aghast and made their feelings well known.

W.E.N. retreated to London for some peace and quiet. He wasn't willing to side against Fanny, but he did give Florence a yearly allowance of 500 pounds. This allowed her to accept the job because she wouldn't be paid. At last Fanny gave up, and Florence accepted the position. Before it started, Florence went to Paris for training. But she came down with the measles soon after arriving. She stayed at Clarkey's house until she had recovered enough to return to England

This time she didn't go home. She rented an apartment in London. She was ready to make her own way in the world.

In August, 1853, thirty-three-year-old Florence Nightingale started her first job. She quickly found that her organizational skills were needed as much as her nursing abilities. The committee that had given her the job hadn't done much to get the hospital ready before Florence took over. They argued with each other and wasted much of the available money.

Florence wasted no time or money in setting things right. She made arrangements to buy supplies more cheaply and outfitted the hospital with whatever she could find, including some of Fanny's old curtains. She got rid of the hospital doctor and hired a different one who could make up his own medicines. That saved on druggist bills.

The committee members were appalled at Florence's take-charge ways. They had anticipated a hard-working, God-fearing superintendent who would accept their guidance without question. Instead, they got a hardheaded, opinionated young woman who had suffered too long from denied dreams. She knew how to do her job and intended to do it whether her methods were ladylike or not.

Within six months the hospital was running smoothly, and Florence was happy. Fanny put aside her disapproval enough to send gifts of flowers, vegetables, and meat from Embley Park. The patients adored their superintendent, who went beyond providing for their medical needs. She found money for them and arranged vacations before they returned to work.

Florence's career was going so well that she started looking for something different, something more challenging. She heard that one of London's major hospitals was going through a reorganization. It needed a nurse training school, and she was just the person to get it off the ground.

Before Florence could turn her full energies to this new task, world events changed the course of her life. An obscure peninsula in Russia would soon make her world-famous.

In the early nineteenth century, poor children who roamed the inner-city streets of London and other cities in England rarely got a chance to go to school. There were charity and Sunday Schools but no public schools. The teachers at the existing schools sometimes complained that these poor children were so ragged, hungry, and dirty that it was impossible to teach them. What were soon called "Ragged Schools" developed to answer the special needs of these thousands of children.

Several men can lay claim to starting the Ragged School movement, but the first one seems to have been started by John Pound in 1818. Pound was a shoemaker in the city of Portsmouth who used his shop as a gathering place for local children. He taught them reading, writing, arithmetic, and religion. He also included instruction in nature study, cooking, toy making, and clothes mending. Pound was known to bribe waterfront children with baked potatoes if they would come to his school.

Ragged schools met in all matter of buildings, including stables, empty storerooms, covered railway arches, and old houses. The teachers were volunteers at first and usually of the working class. Most students were boys but eventually girls were welcomed as well. The students could count on some sort of food and the opportunity to get some decent clothing as well as a basic education.

Lord Shaftesbury was an important force in organizing and expanding the Ragged Schools program in the 1840s. The schools joined together to form the Ragged Schools Union. Lord Shaftesbury served as president of the union for forty years. His social standing helped make the schools a respectable place for the wealthy to support.

More than 350 Ragged Schools were established by 1870, at which time they began to be absorbed into the regular educational system.

Florence became known as "The Lady with the Lamp" because she walked through the hospital wards at night with a lamp checking on the patients. The famous poet Henry Wadsworth Longfellow wrote a poem in 1857 to honor Florence. It was called "Santa Filomena", which is Italian for "Saint Nightingale."

4

The Lady with the Lamp

It's likely that British leaders didn't realize how unprepared their army was for battle. There hadn't been a real war since Napoleon had been defeated in 1815. The army's internal organization had layers upon layers of rules and regulations that were supposed to make it run efficiently. They did just the opposite. The weapons, ammunition, medical supplies, and food that should have accompanied the troops to Crimea disappeared into the bog of official rules.

When fighting began in September, 1854, there was immediately a critical lack of supplies. The dire circumstances might not have been well-known at home in Britain if not for the newspaper reporting done from the front. Graphic reports of the chaos on the battlegrounds stirred the British public to a fever pitch of indignation.

Florence Nightingale was thrust into this boiling pot of public outrage. Her friend Sidney Herbert was now the government official in charge of money for the army. He asked Florence to go to Scutari. He said that this was an opportunity for Florence to show the world how useful nurses could be.

Florence didn't have to be convinced. In fact, she had already decided to make the trip at her own expense. Herbert's offer improved the situation. She recruited her nurses and set out within a week. They crossed the English Channel and took a train to Marseilles.

In spite of the promise of abundant supplies waiting at Scutari, Florence purchased many items on her way. Some of the money came from *The Times* newspaper. Some was her own. Friends had also given her funds to use for the troops.

The supplies that Florence obtained probably did more to insure the success of the experiment than the actual nursing. Nursing care by itself couldn't have stopped the hospital from collapsing. It took the bedding, bandages, food, cookware, shirts, medicines, and endless other items that Florence provided to save the day because the promised supplies were not waiting when they arrived at Scutari.

The weeks after Florence and the nurses went to work were harrowing ones. Thousands of wounded and sick men poured into the two hospitals in Scutari. Many had been lying for days on board ships without food or blankets or treatment.

Florence bought scrub brushes and had the floors cleaned. Sack mattresses were filled with straw and placed on the floors. The sewers weren't working under the hospital, making it necessary for the patients to use chamberpots. The pots were seldom emptied, which meant the whole hospital had a dreadful stench. One of the first difficult jobs she undertook was to persuade the orderlies to empty the chamberpots on a regular schedule.

The newly arrived casualties were washed and their wounds tended before they were laid carefully on the clean mattresses. She set up what was called an "extra-diet" kitchen in the little kitchen in the nurses' rooms. The nurses cooked special soft food for the soldiers who couldn't eat the regular hospital food, which consisted of hard biscuits and tough, stringy chunks of meat. Some were too weak, while others had lost many of their teeth to scurvy. Florence had brought stores of arrowroot, wine, and beef broth from Marseilles. The nurses spoon-fed the sickest of the men and all got some nourishing broth.

At night Florence carried a small lamp and walked among the crude beds to check on her patients and comfort them. The men adored her and attempted to restrain their curses and cries of pain out of respect for her.

When Florence wasn't working directly among the soldiers, she toiled constantly doing paperwork. She wrote endless reports and letters to officials, friends, and the families of the soldiers who died at Scutari.

Conditions had improved In the Barrack Hospital by the early months of 1855. The food was better, the patients cleaner, and they were better clothed. Yet the death rate continued to climb, reaching 42 percent at its peak.

Far more of the men who came to Florence's hospital were sick than were wounded. Even when there weren't battles, sick men continued to flood into the Barrack Hospital. They fell victim to several ailments Including typhus, dysentery, and cholera.

The military doctors and Florence herself at first attributed the high death rate to the horrible conditions that the men had endured In the army camps before being transferred to Scutari. However, statistics showed that a soldier was more likely to live if he remained at the primitive hospitals near the front lines than if he were transferred back to the Barrack Hospital.

In March the British government sent a Sanitary Commission to investigate the conditions of hospital buildings at Scutari and in the Crimea. The results of the investigation were chilling.

The commission found that the sewers running under the Barrack Hospital were poorly constructed, choked with debris, and overloaded. They were essentially open cesspools. Poisonous sewer gases drifted upward through the hospital wards.

Unlike most official commissions, the Sanitary Commission was given authority to correct any problems they encountered. They ordered the water supply channel opened and cleaned. In it they found the carcasses of dead horses. They had the sewers flushed and cleaned. The hospital walls were limewashed. Wooden shelves in the wards that harbored rats were torn out.

A startling decrease in the death rate came almost immediately. It was apparent that the hospital conditions the patients endured played a larger part in their chances of survival than the illnesses or wounds that brought them to the hospital in the first place.

Even when the medical conditions improved, Florence still had plenty of problems to solve. The nurses had been difficult to supervise from the very beginning of their mission.

There were arguments among the different religious groups who had sent nurses. The government also kept trying to send out more nurses even though Florence didn't think she needed or could supervise any additional nurses.

She did think that she should visit the hospitals near the front lines. In May, 1855, she crossed the Black Sea and landed at Balaclava. Unfortunately, she soon became ill with a dangerous fever. She recovered after weeks of sickness and recuperation. This illness started a lifetime of poor health for Florence.

Back at Scutari, Florence dealt with another kind of problem. The recovering men had nothing to do to pass the long days. Eventually Florence helped start schools, a recreation center, and a coffee shop. The soldiers learned to read and write and enjoyed donated games. Their excessive drinking ceased and morale improved.

The rest of 1855 passed with the hospitals still overloaded with patients but no longer in crisis. By fall the war was winding down. Florence's efforts began to be talked about at home in England. Popular songs praised her. She appeared as a mannequin in Madame Tussaud's popular London wax museum. All over the country, newborn baby girls were named for her.

The Crimean War ended in April, 1856. By the end of July Florence had seen the last of her patients depart. It was time for the "lady with the lamp" to go home to England.

Joseph Lister

Many people who required surgery in the nineteenth century ended up dying from infections that occurred after successful operations. Doctors could find no way to stop this high mortality rate. Dr. Joseph Lister built on prior discoveries about bacteria to devise a way to stop post-operative infections and greatly decrease the death rate.

In the 1860s, Lister heard an account of the effects of carbolic acid treatment on sewage in the English town of Carlisle. The carbolic acid not only got rid of the odor but also kept cattle from getting sick when they ate grass in the pasture where the sewage had been spread. Lister later said in his reports, "The applicability of carbolic acid for the treatment of compound fracture naturally occurred to me."[1]

One of Lister's first successes came with the treatment of a boy who had been run over by a wagon. The child's right leg was broken and there was a huge open wound. Lister thought it was hopeless to try to save the boy by normal treatment methods. Instead he used chloroform to put him to sleep and applied carbolic acid to the wound. After treating the fracture, he packed the remaining raw surface with lint soaked in the acid. The lint was then covered with tin foil. When the bandage was changed, the same treatment was reapplied. The boy eventually recovered completely.

Lister soon began using carbolic acid in the operating room as well. He not only applied it to patients' wounds but also sprayed it in the air and on the surgical equipment. The death rate from infection in Lister's hospital fell dramatically.

Lister's use of carbolic acid led to a whole different way of doing surgery. Surgery could be now be performed before it was a last resort because a patient had much better odds of surviving the operation.

A weary and careworn Florence wanted nothing to do with any plans to give speeches or attend meetings after she came home from the Crimean War. She did, however, accept an invitation from Queen Victoria and Prince Albert to visit them at their country home at Balmoral Castle in Scotland.

5

A Long and Useful Life

All of Britain wanted to welcome home their heroine. There were offers of parades with marching bands and speeches. Florence would have nothing to do with such plans. She traveled home secretly.

On August 7, 1856, Florence arrived alone at the railroad station near Lea Hurst. She walked across the fields to see her family. They must have been shocked at her thin, sickly appearance. Indeed it was soon family knowledge that Florence probably wouldn't live much longer.

After her visit at Lea Hurst, Florence moved into rooms in the Burlington Hotel in London. Her mother and sister stayed with her, much to Florence's dismay. They insisted that they were helping the returning heroine but were actually a bother to Florence, who immediately plunged into writing hundreds of pages of government reports and recommendations.

She felt that the entire army medical system had to be changed or men would continue to die needlessly. She analyzed death rates at different hospitals and camps in the Crimea and came to a painful conclusion. Sanitary problems rather than the war had killed so many soldiers. Soon she began a crusade to change the system that allowed such a tragedy to occur.

Florence wanted the government to start a medical school for army doctors and appoint a Royal Commission to investigate the shortcomings of the medical system in the Crimea. This was not a popular idea even among the politicians who agreed with her. They preferred to make changes without the fuss and accusations a Royal Commission would bring.

When Florence threatened to publish her own account of the chaos in the Crimea, the Commission was appointed without delay. She insisted that Sidney Herbert be the commission's chairman. At her request, it also included Dr. John Sutherland, a member of the Sanitary Commission that had cleaned up the Barrack Hospital.

Florence drove the two men mercilessly as they worked on the written portion of the investigation. She disregarded their claims of illness and bullied them back to work. Herbert was especially prone to sickness, but Florence accepted no excuse. If she could work so hard when she was obviously at death's doorstep, then the two men could persevere through minor ailments.

A few weeks before the commission's report was completed in September, 1857, Florence collapsed after complaining of a pounding heart and difficulty breathing. She was forced to rest for awhile. Then she drew up a will and made burial arrangements but continued to work hard and drive those around her. Besides her work on behalf of soldiers, she also wrote about the conditions in public hospitals and sought ways to improve them.

Eventually there was time to plan the nursing school she had wanted to establish. During the war a fund had been set up to honor Florence and her nursing work. Called the Nightingale Fund, it was to be used to start a nursing school. Florence realized that her health might not permit her to run the school, but she could set it up and oversee its operation.

Many of these projects went on at the same time. Florence had a remarkable ability to divide her attention and efforts in more than one direction at once. Reform of the army remained at the top of her list. Sidney Herbert was now head of the War Office and worked tirelessly to make needed changes. Florence saw that reform could come only through her old friend and nagged him constantly to push harder to make improvements. She dismissed his repeated illnesses by saying that the doctors were wrong about Herbert's condition.

Herbert was able to enact many reforms in the army, but his health totally broke down before he could finish. By the summer of 1861 he was dying, but Florence refused to see that he could no longer work. She raged at him for deserting her at a critical time.

When Herbert died on August 2, 1861, Florence was totally shocked. She collapsed in despair and grief. It was weeks before she could resume her work. Florence's reaction to her friend's death paints one of the clearest pictures of her approach to life. She missed Herbert and grieved intensely for him but apparently never felt any remorse that she had driven him to work so hard and long. She never voiced anything other than regret that so much of their reform work died with him.

In the meantime, the Nightingale Training School for Nurses opened in 1860 at St. Thomas Hospital in London. The student nurses were carefully chosen to represent the positive image that Florence wanted for nursing. They signed up for a one-year course followed by three years of hospital duty.

They were instructed according to the principles set out by Florence in *Notes on Nursing*. According to the book, the first rule of nursing a patient was "To keep the air he breathes as pure as the external air, without chilling him."[1] She also wrote that patients needed cleanliness, nourishing food, and quiet surroundings.

The students kept notebooks and attended lectures given by the St. Thomas doctors. They also kept diaries that Florence reviewed monthly. Thirteen nurses graduated from the first class and began their hospital work. Eventually there were nursing schools in several countries that taught their students using the Nightingale Method.

Though Florence took to her bed after Herbert died and remained in poor health for the rest of her life, it became apparent that she wasn't going to die as soon as she and everyone else had thought. She was able to accomplish huge amounts of study and writing while propped up in her bed.

She turned her attention to improving conditions in India, both among the British colonial forces and the native population, even though she never traveled there. A new Indian sanitation committee used many statistics that Florence supplied for a report published in 1863. For many years, it was common for an official newly appointed to India to visit Florence and receive words of wisdom from her before departing.

Student or probationary nurses at Nightingale Training School for Nurses were strictly supervised but each lived in a room by herself with living expenses paid by the Nightingale fund. This photo of a nursing class shows their benefactor seated in the midst of the white-capped student nurses.

Although she never took part in public life again, she traveled to Lea Hurst and Embley Park occasionally. Her parents were in declining health themselves, and it was up to her to handle their affairs. Parthe had married Sir Harry Verney and had her own household to manage.

In 1874 W.E.N. died and Florence took over the complete care of her mother at Lea Hurst. Fanny was blind, and her mind wandered to her younger days. Fanny had caused her daughter much grief in the past, but Florence was able to put her former irritation aside and care tenderly for her mother.

Fanny died in 1880, and Florence moved back to London. Her later years were the most peaceful of her life. She lived in a little house that her father had bought for her in 1865. Her father's heir, Shore Smith, gave her a generous allowance, which she used for small luxuries like fancy meals and entertaining the children of her friends and relatives.

She enjoyed feeding the birds on her balcony and playing with her family of Persian cats. She and Parthe became close again as they had been in childhood. Parthe and her husband lived nearby and the three of them spent much time together.

Members of the government often consulted her about army re-form, public health, and India. She kept a close eye on the nursing school. Each student nurse visited Florence, who assessed her perfor-mance and also asked for any suggestions to improve the school. Flo-rence kept in touch with many of the graduate nurses who were scat-tered throughout Britain and abroad. She sent them flowers, money, and other gifts.

Florence was very proud of the nurses her school had trained. She was adamant that her nurses should be well trained medically but also aware of the spiritual nature of their profession. Florence always consid-ered nursing to be a direct calling from God.

Florence's final years were quiet and peaceful. Her friends and associates died one by one, but she lived to see some of the Indian reforms carried out. In 1907 King Edward VII awarded her the Order of

Merit. One of her country's most prestigious awards, it had never before been given to a woman. By then her mind was lost in wandering. She died peacefully on August 13, 1910.

By the end of Florence's long life, nursing and medicine had changed tremendously since the Crimean War days. In her determination to throw off the ropes that bound a Victorian woman and become a nurse, she had saved countless lives. Florence Nightingale saw problems and set out to solve them. Her energy and persistence have made our lives today better. She is sometimes called the "mother of modern nursing" and rightly so.

Raj is a Hindu word meaning rule. The British Raj refers to the time when Britain ruled India. Britain had maintained trading stations in India from the early 1600s, and the powerful East India Company gradually administered more and more of the country. The Company's rule ended as a result of the Indian Mutiny of 1857.

The Mutiny had complicated causes, but the clash of two cultures was at the heart of the violent uprising against British men, women, and children. The rebels were defeated after a year of savagery and massacres on both sides. The British government stepped in to take over the administration of much of India.

British military officers and other government officials arrived in India with their families to rule a country that had more than 200 million people. The majority of British people thought that their government was doing the Indian people a favor by ruling them. Many reforms and improvements were instituted, but the Indians were paying taxes to a government in which they had no voice.

For most British families who lived there, India during the Raj was a totally alien world. They had dozens of servants, including ayahs-or nannies-for the children. Indians loved children and this fondness led to a charmed existence for the lucky children who often spent more time with their ayahs than their parents. They rode ponies, attended elaborate children's parties and were greatly spoiled by their ayahs. Children usually were sent back to England to attend boarding school and found themselves terribly homesick for their beloved exotic India.

During the early part of the twentieth century, the Indians began clamoring for freedom from British rule. Mohandas K. Gandhi, who believed in non-violent opposition, became the leader of this movement. The Raj finally came to an end in 1947 when the British granted independence to India.

Chronology

1820	Born May 12 in Florence, Italy
1825	Family moves to Embley Park near Portsmouth
1832	W.E.N. begins teaching his daughters himself
1837	Records a call from God in her journal on February 7
1839	Returns from 18 months traveling in Europe
1844	Decides to work with sick in hospitals
1845	Parents reject her plan to train at Salisbury Infirmary
1847	Travels to Italy
1850	Visits Kaiserswerth Institution in Germany
1851	Returns to Kaiserswerth for three months to observe and work
1853	Begins first job as superintendent of Harley Street Hospital
1854	Travels to Turkey with party of nurses to work in Scutari hospitals
1855	Contracts fever and almost dies
1856	Returns to England as a hero after Crimean War ends
1857	Royal Commission finishes work
1859	Publishes *Notes on Hospitals* and *Notes on Nursing*
1860	Nightingale Training School for Nurses opens
1861	Her friend, Sidney Herbert, dies on August 2
1865	Moves into her own house in London given to her by her father
1874	Father dies
1880	Mother dies
1890	Sister Parthe dies
1892	Submits plan for Indian taxes to be used for sanitation
1897	Achievements recognized during Queen Victoria's Diamond Jubilee celebration
1907	Awarded the Order of Merit from King Edward VII
1910	Dies in sleep on August 13

Timeline in Nursing

1836   The modern movement for nursing education begins in the German town of Kaiserswerth.

1849   Elizabeth Blackwell becomes the first woman to receive an M.D. degree from a U.S. medical school.

1854   Florence Nightingale organizes a group of women to serve as nurses in the Crimean War.

1860   The Nightingale Training School for Nurses opens in London.

1861   Dorthea Dix organizes a corps of female nurses to serve in the U.S. Civil War.

1864   French scientist Louis Pasteur proves that infections are caused by germs in the air.

1865   Joseph Lister discovers that carbolic acid can be used to pre vent infection after surgeries.

1887   Ethel Fenwick founds the Royal British Nurses' Association, the world's first professional nurses' association.

1903   North Carolina is the first state to pass a nurse registration law.

1918   Nearly 300 military nurses die while serving during World War I

1919   Public health or visiting nurses number close to 9,000 in America.

1930   First stewardesses begin flying on Boeing 80A transport planes; they are required to be registered nurses.

1945   Approximately 150,000 volunteer nurses' aides serve in hospitals in World War II.

1954   Licensed Practical Nurses number over 144,000 in the United States.

1960   Male nurses account for only one percent of active nurses.

1965   Nursing specialties such as coronary and intensive care emerge.

1984   Graduates of nurse practitioner programs are widely employed.

1994   Advanced-practice nurses such as nurse-midwives and nurse-anesthetists number near 100,000.

2003   The International Council of Nurses announces a campaign to register all new-born babies throughout the world.

2004   Nursing is a well-respected profession throughout the world. In the U.S., the national average income for all nurses is $45,500. May 12, service held in Westminster Abbey to commemorate the life and work of Florence Nightingale.

Chapter Notes

Chapter 1   The Experiment

1. Cecil Woodham-Smith, *Florence Nightingale, 1820-1910* (New York: McGraw Hill Book Company, Inc., 1951), p. 85.

2. ibid., pp. 139-40.

3. David Turner, "War Correspondent William Russell's Blunt Truths about the Crimean War Changed the British Army" *Military History*, 2002), p. 12.

4. ibid., p. 13.

Chapter 2   The Independent Thinker

1. Cecil Woodham-Smith, *Florence Nightingale, 1820-1910* (New York: McGraw-Hill Book Company, Inc., 1951), p. 9.

2. ibid., p. 12.

Chapter 3   The Superintendent

1. Barbara Montgomery Dossey, *Florence Nightingale: Mystic, Visionary, Healer.* (Pennsylvania: Springhouse Corporation, 2000), p. 67-68.

2. Sir Edward Cook, Florence Nightingale: Volume II (London: Macmillan and Co., Limited, 1914), p. 106.

Chapter 4   The Lady with the Lamp

1. Peter Kandela, "Antisepsis," *The Lancet*, (March 13, 1999), p. 1.

Chapter 5   A Long and Useful Life.

1. Victor Skretkowicz, Editor, *Florence Nightingale's Notes on Nursing*, (London: Scutari Press, 1992), p. 21.

2. Collins, David R. *Florence Nightingale: God's Servant at th Battlefield.* Fenton, Michigan: Mott Media, 1985.

3. Colver, Ann. *Florence Nightingale: War Nurse.* Broomall, Pennsylvania: DoChelsea House Publishers, 1992.

Glossary

arrowroot (AIR oh root) starch powder used to make puddings for invalids

barracks (Bare ecks) large building used to house soldiers

cesspool (SAYS pool) an open pit into which untreated sewage drains

chloroform (KLOR uh form) one of the first anesthetics commonly used

invalid (IN vah lid) someone who cannot take care of himself because of illness

mannequin (MAN eh kin) a life-size wax or plaster figure

spa a resort hotel where a person goes to take treatments for health problems

statistics (stah TIS ticks) number facts or data

stump pillow (stump PILL oh) used to support the stump of an arm or leg after amputation

suitor (SUIT ore) boyfriend

For Further Reading

Dossey, Barbara Montgomery. *Florence Nightingale: Mystic, Visionary, Healer*. Springhouse, Pennsylvania: Springhouse Corporation, 2000.

Gorrell, Gena K. *Heart and Soul: The Story of Florence Nightingale*. Plattsburgh, New York:Tundra Books, 2000.

Lorene, Kristi and Ken Save. *Florence Nightingale*. Uhrichsville, Ohio: Barbour Publishing, Inc., 1997.

Malam, John. *Florence Nightingale*. Barrington, Illinois: Heinemann Library, 2001.

Works Consulted

Allen, Charles, Editor. *Plain Tales From the Raj*. New York: St. Martin's Press, 1975.

Battye, Evelyn. *Costumes and Characters of the British Raj*. Exeter, England: Webb & Bower, 1982.

Cook, Sir Edward. *The Life of Florence Nightingale, Volume I*. London: Macmillan and Co., Limited, 1914.

Cook, Sir Edward. *The Life of Florence Nightingale, Volume II*. London: Macmillan and Co., Limited, 1914.

Delgrado, Alan. *Victorian Entertainment*. New York: American Heritage Press,1971.

Dossey, Barbara Montgomery. *Florence Nightingale: Mystic, Visionary, Healer*. Springhouse, Pennsylvania: Springhouse Corporation, 2000.

Goldie, Sue M., Editor. *"I have done my duty": Florence Nightingale in the Crimean War 1854-56*. Iowa City: University of Iowa Press, 1987.

Huxley, Elspeth. *Florence Nightingale*. New York: G. P. Putnam's Sons, 1975.

Kalisch, Philip and Beatrice. *The Advance of American Nursing*. Philadelphia: J.B. Lippincott Company, 1995.

Kandela, Peter. "Antisepsis."*The Lancet*, March 13, 1999.

Margetson, Stella. Leisure and Pleasure in the Nineteenth Century. New York: Coward-McCann, Inc.,1969.

Pool, Daniel. *What Jane Austen Ate and Charles Dickens Knew: From Fox-Hunting to Whist - the Facts of Daily Life in 19th Century England*. New York: Simon & Schuster,1993.

Porter, Roy. The Greatest Benefit To Mankind, A Medical History of Humanity. New York: W.W. Norton & Company, 1997.

Priestley, J.B. *Victoria's Hey day*. New York: Harper & Row, 1972.

Russell, William Howard. *Russell's Despatches from the Crimea*. New York: Hill and Wang, 1966.

Selanders, Louise C. *Florence Nightingale: An Environmental Adaptation Theory*. Newbury Park, California: Sage Publications, 1993.

Skretkowicz, Victor, Editor. *Florence Nightingale's Notes On Nursing.* London: Scutari Press, 1992.

Small, Hugh. *Florence Nightingale, Avenging Angel.* New York: St. Martin's Press, 1998.

Summers, Anne. *Angels and Citizens.* London: Routledge & Kegan Paul, 1988.

The Helen Fuld Health Trust. *The Nurse Theorists Portraits of Excellence: Florence Nightingale.* Oakland, California: Studio Three Productions, 1990.

Turner, David. "War Correspondent William Russell's Blunt Truths about the Crimean War Changed the British Army." *Military History,* December, 2002.

Vicinus, Martha and Bea Nergaard, Editors. *Ever Yours, Florence Nightingale: Selected Letters.* Cambridge, Massachusetts: Harvard University Press, 1990.

Wilson, A.N. *The Victorians.* New York: W.W. Norton & Company, 2003.

Woodham-Smith, Cecil. *Florence Nightingale, 1820-1910.* New York: McGraw-Hill Book Company, Inc., 1951.

On the Internet

The Epic of the Race: India 1857 http://www.geocities.com/ Broadway/Alley/5443indmut.htm

The Charge of the Light Brigade (25 October 1854) http:// www.rickard.karoo.net/ battlesmain7.html

Florence Nightingale: A Treatment http://www/countryjoe.com/ nightingale/treatmt.htm

The History of Ragged Schools http://www.maybole.org/history/ articles/ historyofraggedschools.htm

Note to Researchers

Florence Nightingale wrote thousands of words in letters, reports, and private notes. Many of these documents have been preserved and are located in several collections in London. Although she didn't write an autobiography, she did make some autobiographical notes in the middle of her long life. The first biography of her life was written by Sir Edward Cook and published in 1913. Some documents and letters became available after that and have been included in Cecil Woodham-Smith's biography published in 1951. Several collections of her letters and diaries have also been published. The two biographies mentioned are generally considered the factual basis for most other biographies published since then, but the newer books are somewhat more readable than the first two.

Index